Learn French Like a Native for Beginners - Level 2

Learning French in Your Car Has Never Been Easier! Have Fun with Crazy Vocabulary, Daily Used Phrases, Exercises & Correct Pronunciations

www.LearnLikeNatives.com

© Copyright 2020 By Learn Like A Native

ALL RIGHTS RESERVED

No part of this book may be reproduced, stored in a retrieval system, or transmitted in any form or by any means, without the prior written permission of the publisher.

Content

Let me give you a little glance at what we will be seeing...

Introduction 1

Chapter 1 – Dreaming of the South 13

Chapter 2 – Not Only Birds Can Fly 32

Chapter 3 – Looking for a Ride? 41

Chapter 4 – I Find My Happiness Where the Sun Shines ... 52

Chapter 5 – I Have So Many Stories to Tell You 61

Chapter 6 – So Many Roads and So Many Places 82

Chapter 7 – Eat, Travel, Love 91

Chapter 8 – Sick & Abroad! 99

Chapter 9 – Learn the Ropes 106

Chapter 10 – Bring, Learn & Lead 114

Chapter 11 – New Job, New Life 126

Chapter 12 – Bringing Home the Bacon 135

Conclusion 143

Are you intrigued?

Introduction

Welcome aboard your journey to French fluency!

I'm so glad you're joining the ever-growing family of people who are curious and passionate about this amazing language. Have you always wanted to learn French? Or just caught the bug recently? Either way, you're in the right place. French is an incredible language in so many different ways, and mastering it will give you the keys to a wonderful culture, with deep roots and remarkable history.

French is the official language of 29 countries around the world. Although it's only the 6th most spoken language by the total number of speakers, it's the second most studied language worldwide with more than 120 million current learners.

Beyond its European roots, French is the second most spoken language in Africa behind English, and has native-speaking territories across every single continent. As such, it's an official language of the United Nations and many other international organizations. Finally, according to *Bloomberg Businessweek*, French is the third most useful language for business.

Who would have thought!

Hopefully, these couple of quick facts give you a better picture of the importance of the French language worldwide, today and for times to come.

A Fascinating History

French is a lot more than numbers and figures. It's an immensely rich culture going back more than a thousand years. As a matter of fact, French rulers are amongst the most iconic and recognized historical figures of all time. Louis XIV, Napoleon Bonaparte, William the Conqueror. All these names are deeply ingrained in world culture and imagination, even to this day.

France was the first modern nation-state (after San Marino) and its influence still spans far beyond its domestic borders. Indeed, French has a long history as the international language of culture, literature, and science. It's the language of arts and culture and many say it's the language of love! For centuries, it was the spoken language of the educated elites and the European nobility and aristocracy. Believe or not, even Russian monarchs spoke French.

That's right, the Tsar spoke French at home!

French is therefore an immensely interesting language, deeply grounded in history but also hugely relevant to modern times.

A Traveler's Best Friend

Your recent travels probably exposed you to overcrowded city centers and famous landmarks transformed into stale, money-making amusement parks. What's more insipid than checking monuments off a list for a week-end, surrounded by souvenir shops and restaurant chains? If you're someone yearning for cultural immersion, traveling like that just doesn't cut it.

Speaking the local language has an amazing impact on your adventures abroad. Whether in Paris, Bruxelles, Geneva or Montreal, speaking French will, therefore, allow you to separate yourself from the crowd and experience places the way they're supposed to be.

Thanks to your French skills, you'll avoid the constant flow of noisy, obnoxious (and sometimes badly-behaved) tourists, and venture into local, non-commercial, residential areas. There, you'll be more likely to find what French cities truly have to offer: their customs, traditions, and perhaps more importantly, their people.

Earning respect and friendship of local populations will add a wonderful dimension to your travels and unlock a coveted treasure: human interaction. Your willingness to approach locals in their own language will be appreciated as a mark of respect. You'll find people more inclined to talk to you, help you, and even befriend you.

And with Learn Like A Native, you'll have lots of fun along the way!

A Useful Business Tool

First impressions go a long way. In your search for a job, knowing other languages is a huge advantage that will separate you from the rest of the field. Employers will take your desire and ability to master another language as evidence of your willingness to try new things and see the world from a different perspective. Not only will French look good on your

CV, but it will also highlight your confidence to take on new challenges – a great trait for any potential employee.

Imagine now that your company's biggest client is a French investor, a Parisian businessman or a banker from French-Switzerland. How impressed will your boss be to see you close a huge contract by befriending him through your exquisite French skills? I'd say there's a good chance that your name will come up for the next promotion.

Imagine you discover a huge opportunity in the Monaco market and your contact point is a warm but tough Monégasque man with many options. A friendly relationship with a fellow French-speaker could be the determining factor in his decision to do business with you rather than with someone else. In other words, don't underestimate the power of human contact. Especially in today's globalized world, adding French to your business arsenal is a great way to get ahead of the pack, put yourself in favorable situations and create opportunities that just wouldn't exist otherwise.

The Perfect Method

I'm sure you've been told there's no right or wrong way to learn a language. Well, that can't be right, because it's wrong! The truth is, most people don't lack in motivation, drive, excitement, determination, or even talent. More than anything, people lack the correct method.

I've been learning and teaching languages my whole life, and I've realized that the number one reason why people get stuck learning any language is simple. It's not because they are lazy, it's not because they don't have time, it's because they are bored!

You could go to the best schools and have the best teachers in the world, but if you're bored in your French class, you're unlikely to get anywhere. Starting from scratch and ingesting new knowledge and can be a daunting thing as it is. So, if you're not fully engaged, learning a new language will be a long road.

Think about it. You've been a child before. Did you learn grammar before you knew how to speak? Of course not! So why do that now? In my opinion, that's where most language methods fail. Because they get caught up in all the specific rules and formal details, before worrying if their students understand what's going on. What's the point of knowing irregular verbs, if you can't even order food at the restaurant!

My point being, unless you're planning to write a Ph.D. in French, the most important thing for you is to be able to speak with other people.

That's where Learn Like A Native comes in!

With approximately 120 million people who speak and study French as a non-native language, there's plenty of opinions as to what the best way to learn is.

That's why I based my method on modern expert research. The latest studies show that the most efficient way to learn languages – and French in particular – is by learning vocabulary and grammar in conversation.

Using this method, I'll teach you how to apply formal knowledge in a real-life environment, through practical and relatable materials. With short and fun lessons, you'll stay engaged every step of the way, helping you retain vocabulary much more efficiently.

The audiobook version is narrated by a French native speaker who will get you comfortable with the sounds of the language. You'll take an active part in the learning process and be required to speak, repeat and exercise new sounds as they come up throughout the lessons.

If you have any trouble, the textbook will help you with written sounds so you can visualize letters and the sound they relate to.

You'll feel like you're in a French class. But one you can take everywhere! With only 20 to 30 minutes per lesson, you can focus on each topic independently without any stress. Squeeze them into your schedule, sitting in your car or waiting for the Bus, and enjoy the flexibility of going through each step at your own pace. No one is watching you, of course, but I trust you'll do the work! Before you know it, you'll find yourself having a full-blown conversation in French and wonder how you got there!

It's fun, easy-to-use, and most importantly, it works!

www.LearnLikeNatives.com

www.LearnLikeNatives.com

FREE BOOK!

Get the *FREE BOOK* that reveals the secrets path to learn any language fast, and without leaving your country.

Discover:

- The **language 5 golden rules** to master languages at will

- Proven **mind training techniques** to revolutionize your learning

- A complete step-by-step guide to **conquering any language**

www.LearnLikeNatives.com

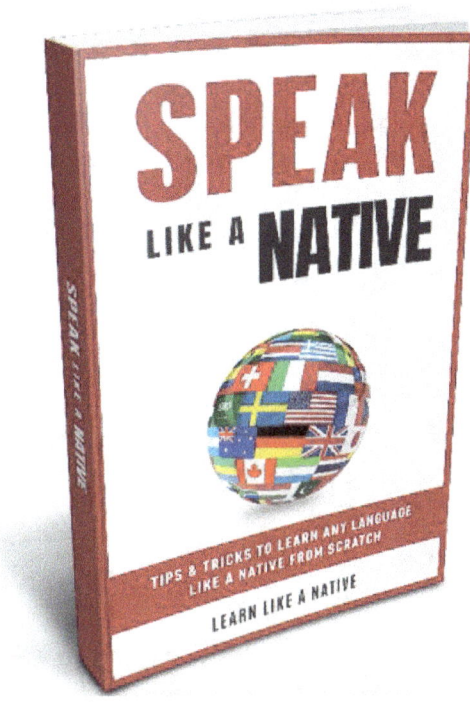

www.LearnLikeNatives.com

www.LearnLikeNatives.com

Chapter 1 – Dreaming of the South

You are sitting at home, thinking about vacation, and suddenly a friend calls you to tell you about their latest family travel to the famous "Côte d'Azur" – it was a beautiful, sunny, diverse and entertaining place. You hang up and start imagining yourself with a glass of Chardonnay in hand, the sea in front of you.

Can you imagine shopping with your family through the little streets of world-renowned Cannes? Can you feel the hand of your loved one, the touch, while enjoying a glass of wine at sunset? Just stay with me, because you can have it all.

To make this a reality, the first thing you need to search for are requirements, hotels, and transportation.

English	French
To travel	Voyager
I want **to travel** to Montreal.	Je veux voyager à Montréal.

Vwa-ya-jé

Notice the "oy" sound. For the French language, "oy" or "oi" is almost always pronounced as "wa".

Now repeat: Vwa-ya-jé.

Requirements	Exigences
Requirements to travel to France.	**Les exigences** pour voyager en France.

Eh-guh-zee-gen-suh

Travel stuff	Affaires de voyage

| I will need to go buy some travel stuff. | J'aurais besoin d'aller acheter des **affaires de voyage.** |

Ah-fer-duh-vwa-ya-guh

This is a typical "difficult" word for English speakers because French has a different "r" sound.

Many French students have trouble with the letter *r*. Follow step-by-step instructions to learn how to pronounce the French *r*:

1. Open your mouth.

2. Close your throat as if you're going to gargle or to avoid swallowing a mouthful of liquid, and say "k" carefully, several times.

3. Pay attention to where in your throat the *k* sound is made. We'll call this the K place.

4. Begin slowly closing your throat until you can almost feel the K place. Your throat should be only partially constricted.

5. Tense the muscles around the K place.

6. Gently push air through your partially-constricted throat.

7. Practice saying "ra-ra-ra" (where r = steps 4-6) every day.

Back to requirements--checking this is very important: due to political and health challenges in many countries, it is possible that you may need some extra requirements to visit, such as vaccines or a travel visa.

Visa	Visa
Do I need a **visa** to travel to France?	Est-ce que j'ai besoin d'un visa pour voyager en France?

Please notice how the word "visa" is the same in both languages, as well as its pronunciation.

Next phrase.

Vaccines	Vaccins

Vaccines are needed to visit French Islands.	Certains **vaccins** sont nécessaires afin de visiter les îles Françaises.

Vak-ssen

"Vaccines" translates as "vaccins", which is almost similar in the written form. However, the pronunciation is not quite the same. This word can be split into two syllables: "vak-ssen".

In case you have these requirements covered, the next step would be to look for flights.

Most airline platforms are multilingual. However, it is known that some domestic flights could be cheaper when bought with a national airline.

Airlines	Compagnies aériennes
What **airlines** travel to Nice?	Quelles **compagnies aériennes** vont à Nice?

Com-pa-nee a-é-ree-ehn-uh

Something to keep in mind is that vowels in French are very open and clear. For example, a French "e" always has a similar sound as the one you would use to say "essay". That starting "e" sound is what we are looking for.

Flights	Vols
Find **flights** from New-York to Paris.	Trouver des **vols** de New-York à Paris.

"vol". The "s" is not pronounced here.

You can notice how the word "from" translates to "de", which is your starting point. While your destination is covered by "à".

One-way trip	Un aller simple
Do you want a **one-way trip**?	Voulez-vous un **aller simple**?

Al-eh sem-pluh

Round trip	Un aller-retour
No, I want a **round trip**.	Non. Je voudrais un **aller-retour**.

Al-eh ruh-toor

Dates	Dates
Dates for your travel?	Les **Dates** de votre voyage?

Repeat after me: Da-tuh. Once again, the "s" is not pronounced.

When looking for accommodations, you have many great references at your disposal, but it is always preferable to ask the locals for specifics related to the best and most touristy locations.

To stay	Loger
Best places **to stay** in Paris.	Les meilleurs endroits où **loger** à Paris.

Lo-jeh

Touristic	Touristique(s)
Most **touristic** places in France.	Les endroits les plus **touristiques** en France.

Too-ree-stee-kuh

Once you have found somewhere you like, the next step is to book a room.

To Book	Réserver
I want to **book** a room.	Je veux **réserver** une chambre.

As you can see, this is another word where you need to put your "r" into training. Repeat after me: reh-zer-veh.

Good! Are we acing those r's or what?

Depending on how many people you include in your trip, you could choose a single room or a double room.

Single room	Chambre simple
I want a **single room**.	Je veux une **chambre simple**.

Sham-bruh sem-pluh

Double room	Chambre double.

| I want a **double room**. | Je veux une **chambre double**. |

Sham-bruh doo-bluh

If you do not enjoy flying, perhaps other transportation methods could be useful.

Cruise	Croisière
I want to go on a **cruise** in the Mediterranean.	Je veux aller en **croisière** dans la Méditerranée.

Crwa-zieh-ruh

How do you feel, so far? Ready to book a trip?

Great! Because now we are going to do some packing.

First, the verb that makes it happen: to pack.

To pack	Faire une valise
I need to **pack** my baggage.	Je dois **faire ma valise**.

Fehr ma va-lee-zuh

There is no actual word for "packing" in French, when it comes to packing a suitcase: Here, the literal translation would be "do a suitcase, or do my suitcase".

With this in mind, repeat again: Je dois faire ma valise.

Of course, you need a suitcase.

Suitcase	Valise
I need a bigger **suitcase**.	J'ai besoin d'une **valise** plus grande.

Va-lee-zuh

The word "valise" can be used in general. However, similar to English, French distinguishes a difference between your checked bags and your carry-on.

Checked bag	Bagage en soute
Your ticket includes one **checked bag**.	Votre ticket inclut un **Bagage en soute**.

Bah-gaj an soo-tuh

Carry-on	Bagage à main

Your **carry-on** is too big.	Votre **bagage à main** est trop grand.

Ba-gaj a mein

Now there is an open suitcase on your bed. It's time to pack!

Shirt	Chemise
I like this **shirt** for the trip.	Cette **chemise** est bien pour le voyage.

Shuh-mee-zuh

T-shirt	T-shirt
Why don't you bring a **t-shirt**? Something more sporty.	Pourquoi ne prendrais-tu pas un **t-shirt**? Quelque chose de plus sportif.

Pants	Pantalon

Should I bring some long **pants**?	Devrais-je enmener un **pantalon** long?

Pan-tah-lon

Shorts	Panta-courts
Maybe I should pack some **shorts**.	Je devrais peut-être enmener des **panta-courts**.

Pan-tah koor

Due to globalization, "shorts" is a common way to call short pants, even in French-speaking countries. Just in case, you have the neutral French way.

Skirt/Dress	Jupe/Robe
I think I will pack a **skirt** and maybe a **dress**.	Je crois que je vais enmener une **jupe** et peut-être une **robe**.

Skirt: ju-puh

Dress: ro-buh

www.LearnLikeNatives.com

Sweater	Pull
I will bring a **sweater**.	Je vais enmener un **pull**.

Underwear	Sous-vêtements
Pack **underwear** for a week.	Prends des **sous-vêtements** pour une semaine.

Soo-veh-tuh-men

Socks	Chaussettes
How many **socks** should I bring?	Combien de **chaussettes** devrais-je prendre?

Shoh-set

And, because we are already on it, it is a good idea to go through some body parts.

Feet	Pieds

| You have very cold **feet**. | Tu as des **pieds** très froids. |

Pee-eh

| Legs | Jambes |
| I have to shave my **legs**. | Je dois me raser les **jambes**. |

Jam-buh

| Hands | Mains |
| Do not forget the **hand** cream. | N'oublies pas la crème pour les **mains**. |

mein

| Arms | Bras |
| I want to tan my **arms**. | Je veux bronzer des **bras**. |

brah

| Head | Tête |

| I got a bump on my **head**. | J'ai une bosse sur la **tête**. |

Teh-tuh

Face	Visage
I need a **face** towel.	J'ai besoin d'une serviette pour mon **visage**.

Vee-zag

How are you doing so far? Are there any words you need to repeat?

Before moving on to a little conversation to practice our first lesson, we should briefly speak about the use of the formal form "Vous". While in English there is no difference between formal and informal, French has a separate form to address others in formal situations. For example, at the doctor, restaurant, when talking to the elderly or addressing strangers. In these cases and any other time you need to show respect or want to be polite, you will use "Vous".

As you will see, it is really easy to create the formal version: all you need to do is conjugate the verb at the second person plural (Vous), instead than using the second person singular (Tu).

To start with, we are looking at a conversation between you and a travel agent. In this example, we will use "Vous" in its formal version.

Agent: *Good afternoon! Where do you want to travel?*

Bonjour! Où souhaîtez-vous partir?

Allen: *Nice, France.*

Nice, France.

Agent: *Date for your travel?*

La date de départ?

Allen: *December, 15th.*

Le quinze Décembre.

Agent: *How many adults are traveling?*

Pour combien d'adultes?

Allen: *Two, please.*

Deux, s'il-vous-plaît.

Agent: *Are you traveling with kids?*

Est-ce que vous voyagez avec des enfants?

Allen: *Yes. Two kids.*

Oui. Deux enfants.

Agent: *Would you like a one-way trip or a round trip?*

Souhaitez-vous un aller simple ou un aller-retour?

Allen: *Round trip. Thank you.*

Un aller-retour. Merci.

Agent: *When do you wish to come back?*

Quel jour souhaitez-vous revenir?

Allen: *January, 2nd.*

Le deux Janvier.

Agent: *Okay. Our lowest fare is $350 per person, but it does not include checked bags. Would you like to add checked bags?*

D'accord. Notre tarif le plus bas est de $350 par personne, mais ça n'inclut pas de bagages en soute. Voulez-vous en rajouter ?

Allen: *Not at the moment. Thank you.*

Pas pour le moment, merci.

Agent: *Very well. Would you like to book accommodations?*

Très bien. Voulez-vous réserver des chambres?

Allen: *Sure. What do you have?*

Bien-sûr! Qu'est-ce-que vous avez?

Agent: *I can offer you two bedrooms. One double with a King size bed, and another double with two single beds.*

Je peux vous proposer deux chambres. Une double avec un grand lit double, et une autre avec deux lits simples.

Allen: *Great!*

Super!

Agent: *Perfect. Please, wait in line for a second so I can write down your details.*

Parfait. Veuillez-patienter une seconde pour que je puisse noter vos coordonnées.

How was this for you? Are you feeling more confident now? I hope you do, because we are going to the airport: we have got a plane to catch!

Chapter 2 – Not Only Birds Can Fly

In my experience, airports can be stressful places for multiple reasons. They are crowded spaces with many lines to wait in and documents to show, and you have to do it every single time. Thankfully, I am here to help you be at your gate in time, stress-free.

Let's start by checking you into your flight.

| Passport | Passeport |

Can I please have your **passport?**	Puis-je voir votre passeport?

Pass-por

The check in desk, offers the ideal opportunity to practice what we learned in chapter one. They are going to ask you where you are traveling to, how many people are traveling with you and the number of bags you wish to check in. Unfortunately, overweight luggage is also a VERY frequent problem.

Overweight	Excédent de bagage.
This piece of luggage is **overweight.**	Ce baggage excède le **poids limité**.

Pwah lee-mee-teh

If you managed to avoid the overweight charges—which I hope, as those fees are usually very high—you are ready to go through security controls.

Tray	Panier

| Please take off shoes, coats, and metal objects, and put your belongings in a **tray**. | S'il-vous-plaît, retirez vos chaussures, vos manteaux et tout objets en métal, et mettez vos affaires dans un **panier**. |

Pa-nee-eh

Screen	Révision
Please, go to the left for a second **screen**.	S'il-vous-plaît, dirigez vous à gauche pour une seconde **révision**.

Re-vee-seeon

Once past the security checks, it is time to find your gate.

Gate	Porte d'embarquement
Where is **gate** 15?	Où est la **porte d'embarquement** numéro 15?

Pohr-tuh dem-bahr-kuh-men

| Flight | Vol |

| What **flight** are you taking? | Quel **vol** prenez-vous? |

| Boarding pass | Carte d'embarquement |
| Please, have your **boarding pass** and passport in hand. | Veuillez avoir votre **carte d'embarquement** et votre passeport à proximité, s'il vous-plaît. |

Kar-tuh dem-bahr-kuh-men

| Seat | Siège |
| My **seat** is 23F. | Mon siege est le 23F. |

Sieh-guh

| Bathroom | Salle de bain |
| Is that **bathroom** occupied? | Est-ce que la **salle de bain** est occupée? |

Sal-duh-bein

Blanket	Couverture
Can I have a **blanket**?	Puis-je avoir une **couverture**?

Koo-ver-tur

You know. I could teach you how to ask for other stuff… like some wine? Which is "vin", but let's be responsible and learn some emergency signals.

Go through	Passer
I need to **go through**.	Je dois **passer**.

Pah-seh

Feeling sick	Se sentir malade
I am feeling **sick**.	Je me sens **malade**.

Mah-lah-duh

"Sick" translates directly as "malade". So, work on your phrasing, but especially remember that word, "ma-la-duh". Hearing "sick" in any language is a sign for help.

Headache	Mal de tête
I have a **headache**.	J'ai un **mal de tête**.

Mal duh tet

Fever	Fièvre
I have a **fever**.	J'ai de la **fièvre**.

Fee-eh-vruh

Nausea	Nausée
I feel **nauseous**.	Je me sens **nauséeux/nauséuse**. (if you're a woman)

No-zé-euh / No-zé-euh-zuh

Allergic	Allergique
I am **allergic** to...	Je suis **allergique** à...

Ah-ler-gee-kuh

Obviously, I really hope you won't need to use any of these words, but it's better to be prepared for even unpleasant situations.

What are your thoughts so far? Look at everything that we have just learned. Now you will be able to speak with the airport staff, catch a plane, enjoy a movie, and land safely. Join me for a little dialogue.

Flight Attendant: *Hello! Boarding pass, please.*

Bonjour! Carte d'embarquement, s'il-vous-plaît.

Cris: *Hello!*

Bonjour!

Flight Attendant: *Welcome! You're at seat 14F. By the window.*

	Bienvenue! Votre siège est le 14F. Près de la fenêtre.
Cris:	*Thanks!*
	Merci!
Flight Attendant:	*What would you like to drink today?*
	Que voulez-vous boire?
Cris:	*I would like some water with ice.*
	J'aimerais avoir de l'eau avec des glaçons.
Flight Attendant:	*Of course! Anything else I can do for you?*
	Bien-sûr! Est-ce-que je peux faire autre chose pour vous?
Cris:	*Yes, I am actually feeling a little sick.*
	Oui, Je me sens un peu malade.
Flight Attendant:	*What are your symptoms?*
	Quels sont vos symptômes?
Cris:	*I have a headache and a slight fever.*
	J'ai mal à la tête et un peu de fièvre.

Flight Attendant:	*Are you allergic to something?*
	Etes-vous allergique à quelque chose?
Cris:	*Only to aspirin.*
	Seulement à l'aspirine.
Flight Attendant:	*Ok. Please let me get help.*
	D'accord. Permettez-moi d'aller chercher de l'aide.

Yes, I know what you are thinking. I have chosen the sick-person situation as an example. But how can you blame me? After all, I warned you that this book has been studied for you to feel confident in any situation! How is your head? Are you feeling any better? Not yet? Don't worry. We are landing now.

Chapter 3 – Looking for a Ride?

Welcome to the holiday you always dreamed about! There's just one more thing you will have to worry about before you can enjoy a refreshing drink next to the Eiffel Tower: how to get to your hotel. And so, the time has come to test your knowledge. Now that you arrived at your destination, your super-intensive-Italian immersion is about to start. How exciting is that?

First, let's begin with some basic words.

Taxi	Taxi
I need a **taxi**.	J'ai besoin d'un **taxi**.

Same word? 1 point for globalization!

Shuttle	Navette
Where can I get a **shuttle** to the Hilton Paris Opera?	Ou est-ce que je peux prendre la **navette** pour le Hilton Opera Paris?

Nav-veh-tuh

Bus	Bus
Where can I take a **bus** downtown?	Ou est-ce que je peux prendre un **bus** dans le centre?

Remember, the sound for the French "u" doesn't exist in English. The closest sound we have in English is OU as in "soup".

If you are traveling with family, you are possibly thinking about driving around. We should take you to a car rental.

Rent a car	Louer une voiture
I want to **rent a car**.	Je veux **louer une voiture**.

Vwa-tuu-ruh

Driver's license	Permis de conduire
I will need a **driver's license**.	J'aurai besoin d'un **permis de conduire**.

Per-mi duh con-dwi-ruh

You finally made it to your hotel. The panorama is wonderful and your room has a nice view all over Paris. Can you imagine it? Great! Me too! You will be able to get some rest soon. But, first, you have to check-in.

Check-in	Check in
I would like to **check into** my room.	J'aimerais faire le **check in** de ma chambre.

As you can see, check-in is used in French as well, and it's pronounced in the same way.

Reservation	Réservation
Under what name is the reservation?	Sous quel nom est la **réservation?**

Reh-zer-vah-ssion

Key	Clef
Here is your **key**.	Voici votre **clef**.

Klé (Here, you don't pronounce the "f".)

This is going to depend on what type of hotel you stay in. They now have keycards (clefs magnétiques), or you can even access by pin code (code). In any case, you can use the general word "clef", and everyone will understand.

Elevator	Ascenseur
The **elevator** is down the hall.	L' **ascenseur** se trouve au bout du couloir.

ah-sen-seur

Floor	Etage
Our room is on the 7th **floor**.	Notre chambre se trouve au 7ème **étage**.

This one sounds like "é-ta-guh".

Hey! I know you are eager to get into your room, so let's go in.

Hey! I know you can't wait to see your room, so come on, open the door!

Look around your room. I am sure there is a nice comfy bed, maybe a flat-screen, and a closet. You stop a minute to admire the sunset from your window. But now it's time to learn the name of the things around you.

Bed	Lit
Honey! Our **bed** is huge!	Chéri! Notre **lit** est énorme!

Once again, the "t" doesn't pronounce itself. "lee"

TV	Télévision/ TV

Is it a smart **TV**?	Est-ce-qu'il s'agit d'une smart **TV**?

Closet	Armoire
I'll put the suitcases in the **closet**.	Je vais mettre les valises dans l'**armoire**.

Ar-mwah-ruh.

Go inside your bathroom. Given that bathrooms go with water, and water leaks, you want to pay attention to the following words and phrases in case you have to report any problems with the pipes.

Shower	Douche
We have a massage **shower**.	Nous avons une **douche** hydromassante.

Doo-shuh. I know what you are thinking, this sounds like another word I know. Keep in mind that in French, the "ch" sound is similar to the "sh" one.

Toilet	Toilettes
Two bathrooms! We have a **toilet** each.	Deux salles-de-bains! Nous avons chacun nos **toilettes**.

Twa-let

Sink	Lavabo
I will put some things by the **sink.**	Je vais mettre des affaires à côté du **lavabo**.

La-va-boh

Towels	Serviettes
Hello! I need more **towels**.	Bonjour! J'aurais besoin de plus de **serviettes**.

Ser-vee-et

Pillows	Coussins

| I also need 2 more **pillows**. | J'aurais aussi besoin de deux **coussins** de plus. |

Koo-sen

It turns out my girlfriend uses four pillows, and I always use extra towels. These two are basic survival for us.

Also, some hotels don't put mini-fridges inside the bedrooms anymore. In case you have any requests, follow me to the next phrase.

Mini fridge	Mini-réfrigirateur
I would like a **mini-fridge** in my bedroom.	J'aimerais avoir un **mini-réfrigérateur** dans ma chambre.

You know the word for "mini". Let's practice the hard one:

Ré-fri-ge-ra-tuhr

Mini-réfrigérateur

You have a nice bedroom in there! So, how about some practice?

Concierge: *Hello! How can I help you?*

Bonjour! Comment puis-je vous aider?

Dan: *Hello! I think my sink is leaking.*

Bonjour! Je pense que mon lavabo coule.

Concierge: *I will send someone right away!*

Je vais vous envoyer quelqu'un tout de suite!

Dan: *Thanks. I appreciate your help.*

Merci pour votre aide.

Concierge: *I am sorry for the inconvenience. Is there anything I can do to make your stay more pleasant?*

Je suis désolé pour le désagrément. Est-ce que je peux faire quelque chose pour rendre votre séjour plus agréable?

Dan: *Now that you mention it, I notice my room does not have a mini-fridge.*

Maintenant que vous le mentionnez, je vois qu'il n'y a pas de mini-réfrigérateur dans ma chambre.

Concierge: *Of course! Anything else?*

Bien-sûr, je m'en occupe. Autre chose?

Dan: *I'd like a couple more towels, and one extra pillow, please.*

J'aimerais avoir deux serviettes supplémentaires, et un coussin, s'il vous plait.

Concierge: *Sure! Just in case you need more pillows, you have an extra inside the closet.*

Bien-sûr! Juste au cas ou, si vous avez besoin de coussins supplémentaires, vous en avez un dans l'armoire.

Dan: *Good to know! Thanks!*

C'est bon à savoir! Merci!

Concierge: *Is there anything else I can do for you today?*

Est-ce que je peux faire autre chose pour vous?

Dan: *I am okay. Thank you very much.*

Non tout vas bien. Merci beaucoup.

Concierge: *I will send all that right away. Again, sorry for the inconvenience.*

Je vous envoie tout ça immédiatement. Encore une fois, navré pour le désagrément.

Dan: *It is all good. Thanks for your help.*

C'est tout bon. Merci pour votre aide.

Concierge: *Thank you for being our guest!*

Merci à vous, d'être notre client!

Good! I think we are all set! Ready to go work on your tan?

Chapter 4 – I Find My Happiness Where the Sun Shines

You are finally here, where you have always dreamed to be. The weather is wonderful, and the sounds of church bells ringing are amplified in your room. A small orchestra is playing in the distance. This is all you ever wanted, and now you are ready to go out and discover everything that this amazing place has to offer.

Before heading out, let's check the weather.

Weather	Climat
How's the **weather** in Paris?	Comment est le **climat** à Paris?

Klee-mah

First, just a quick check-up on the seasons.

Spring	Printemps
Flowers are blooming. **Spring** is here.	Les fleurs fleurissent. C'est le **printemps.**

Pren-tam

Summer	été
In the tropics, it always feels like **summer**.	Dans les tropiques, on se sent toujours en **été**.

é-té

Fall	Automne

| Look at the trees, and their **fall** colors. | Regardez les arbres, et leurs couleurs **d'automne**. |

Oh-toh-nuh

As you know, the weather can change quickly. Generally, summer is hot and dry, while winter is cold, but sometimes the weather can change many times a day.

Cloud	Nuage
Look at that big **cloud**.	Regardez ce gros **nuage.**

Nu-ah-guh

Sun	Soleil
The **sun** was too strong.	Le **soleil** tappait trop fort.

So-ley

Rain	Pluie
The **rain** came without a warning.	La **pluie** est arrivée d'un coup.

Plu-ee

Storm	Tempête
Before we knew, the **storm** was here.	Avant même de réaliser, la **tempête** était là.

Is there any popular movie you can think of? I can remember quite a few.

Wind	Vent
The **wind** was so strong that the windows were moving.	Le **vent** était tellement fort que les fenêtres bougaient.

Degrees	Degrés
It was under 0 **degrees**.	Il faisait moins de 0 **degrés**.

Duh-gré

Something to keep in mind is that the metric system is common outside the US. Depending on your destination, having a unit converter could be very useful.

Hurricane	Ouragan
The **hurricane** wrecked it all.	L'**ouragan** a tout détruit.

Ooh-rah-guan. It's the perfect word to practice your "r" sound with.

Sunglasses	Lunettes de soleil
I left my **sunglasses** on the bed!	J'ai laissé mes **lunettes de soleil** sur le lit!

Lu-né-tuh de so-ley

Hat	Châpeau
That's a nice **hat**!	Ce **châpeau** est sympa!

Sha-poh

Sunscreen	Crème solaire
Did you bring **sunscreen**?	As-tu amené de la **crème solaire**?

Crem soh-ler

Umbrella	Parapluie
Let's get under that **umbrella**.	Allons en dessous de ce **parapluie**.

pah-rah-pluee

Raincoat	Imperméable
It is necessary to bring your **raincoat**.	C'est indispensable d'emmener son **imperméable**.

In-per-meh-ah-bluh

This is a very useful word. It is used to indicate a raincoat or just to indicate that something is waterproof: "Impermeabile". Keep it in mind! You may want to get one next time you go shopping.

Talking about shopping, why don't we go for a little spree?

Seller: Hello! Good afternoon. How can I help you?

Bonjour! Comment puis-je vous aider?

Ken: Hey! Good afternoon. I would like to buy some things.

Bonjour! J'aimerais acheter plusieures choses.

Seller: Sure! What do you have in mind?

Bien-sûr! Qu'avez-vous en tête?

Ken: Everything. I need an umbrella, sunglasses, a raincoat... everything.

Tout. J'ai besoin d'un parapluie, de lunettes de soleil, d'un imperméable... tout.

Seller: Oh, I see. Did the hurricane catch you off guard?

Oh, je vois. Vous avez été surprise par l'ouragan?

Ken: Yes. Totally. It's been crazy. Sun goes, and rain comes. Repeatedly.

Oui, totalement. C'est dingue. Le soleil part, la pluie arrive. Constamment.

Seller: *I am sorry to hear that. I will help you gladly.*

Je suis désolé de l'entendre. C'est mon plaisir de vous assister.

Ken: *Thanks! What raincoats do you have?*

Merci! Vous avez quoi comme imperméables?

Seller: *I have these raincoats. Good quality and they protect you down to 0 degrees.*

J'ai ceux-ci. Ils sont de bonne qualité et vous protègent jusqu'à 0 degrés.

Ken: *Awesome! What about umbrellas?*

Super! Qu'en-est-il des parapluies?

Seller: *I have many. It depends on what size you are looking for.*

J'en ai beaucoup. Cela dépend de quelle taille vous recherchez.

Ken: *Just a couple of small umbrellas. Something easy to carry.*

Juste deux petits parapluies. Quelque chose de facile à porter.

Seller: *Sure! Why don't you come with me to pick sunglasses?*

D'accord! Vous voulez venir avec moi pour choisir des lunettes de soleil?

Ken: *Glad to! I will follow you.*

Avec Plaisir! Je vous suis.

Seller: *Very well. This way, please.*

Très bien. Par ici, s'il-vous-plaît.

I hope you have sunscreen. The rain is finally gone, so we are going to some touristy places in a little while and I do not want you to get a nasty sunburn. Remember to bring all your equipment. As always, the most important thing is to be prepared.

Chapter 5 – I Have So Many Stories to Tell You

Do you know what I love most about life in general? The stories! And this is especially true for traveling, because it is all about learning new cultures, meeting new and different people, and facing things you never thought you would.

I remember being in this beautiful sunny place in a little old town in the south of France, not far from the Spanish border. Everything looked perfect. The location was terrific; it was close to everything I needed, and the architecture in our hotel was breathtakingly beautiful. The price was good. Everything was perfect... until I got to my room and found out my toilet was inside the shower.

Trust me, I am not picky. I decided to stay there for the night because the location was amazing and the hotel had already been paid for. I have to admit, though, that all optimism vanished after I went to the bathroom in the middle of the night and got my socks wet from the shower. Needless to say, it was a GREAT and funny story to tell my friends and one of those things I will remember forever.

If you are a storyteller, as I am, then you need a few more tools so you can delight your friends—even your newest local friends—with the fantastic things you have gone through. For that, we will use two different verbal forms to help you bring your story to life. You know this, or at least you may have heard of it back in school. Don't worry. We promised no grammar, okay? I want to show you some examples.

First, let's go through the first one: past simple, which in French, we call "passé simple".

However, the passé simple isn't used often anymore. Therefore, the more appropriate one would be the "passé composé" meaning the composed past.

Why "composed"? Because it is composed of "avoir" (to have) or "être" (to be) + the main verb.

Here, you have to conjugate only "to be" or "to have", while the termination of the main verb remains the same. Easy, right?

Let me explain: The past participle is formed by adding the following endings to the verb stem:

- *é* for verbs ending in *-er*
- *i* for the majority of verbs ending in *-ir*

- *u* with verbs like *attendre, boire, voir, lire,* etc.
- *it* or *is* with verbs like *écrire, dire, prendre,* etc.

The past participle is used to form compound tenses (*passé composé, plus-que-parfait, passif,* etc) with the auxiliary verbs *être* and *avoir*.

We'll start with a verb we know, "voyager"- to travel. Remember how we conjugate the verb "avoir" - "to have". This will give you the opportunity to revise it, in case you have forgotten it.

The participle passé always remains the same.

To travel	Voyager	Root	Termination
I traveled	J'ai voyagé	Voyag-	Er changes to "é"
You traveled	Tu as voyagé		Er changes to "é"
He/She/ traveled	Il/elle a voyagé		Er changes to "é"
We traveled	Nous avons voyagé		Er changes to "é"
You traveled	Vous avez voyagé		Er changes to "é"

They traveled	Ils/elles ont voyagé		Er changes to "é"

See? It's not that difficult right? You just need to remember the conjugation of "Avoir", and then the verb remains the same!

Let's go for a quick practice.

I traveled to France last year.	J'ai voyagé en France l'année dernière.
She traveled through the entire continent.	Ella a voyagé à travers tout le continent.
You traveled a lot the last two months.	Tu as beaucoup voyagé les deux derniers mois.
We traveled to Mexico during the summer.	Nous avons voyagé au Mexique durant l'été.

Can you see? In every sentence, all the actions have already happened: last year, last summer, the last two months.

To eat	Manger	Root	Termination
I ate	J'ai mangé	Mang-	Er changes to "é"
You ate	Tu as mangé		Er changes to "é"
He/She ate	Il/Elle a mangé		Er changes to "é"
We ate	Nous avons mangé		Er changes to "é"
You ate	Vous avez mangé		Er changes to "é"
They ate	Ils ont mangé		Er changes to "é"

Let's practice with some sentences.

You ate the entire cake.	Tu as mangé le gâteau en entier.
She ate only a piece of cake.	Elle a mangé seulement un morceau du gâteau.

We ate one piece each.	Nous avons mangé un morceau chacun.
They ate the rest of the cake.	Ils ont mangé le reste du gâteau.

This is important for stories–everyone has to eat! Also, as seen, it is a good verb to help solve some family culinary disputes.

Same goes for verbs with the "ir" termination, such as "finir":

To finish	Finir	Root	Termination
I finished	J'ai fini	Fin-	Ir changes to "i"
You finished	Tu as fini		Ir changes to "i"
He/She finished	Il/Elle a fini		Ir changes to "i"
We finished	Nous avons fini		Ir changes to "i"
You finished	Vous avez fini		Ir changes to "i"
They finished	Ils/Elles ont fini		Ir changes to "i"

Are you getting closer? Let's go for some practice.

You finished your homework.	Tu as fini tes devoirs.
He finished his shift.	Il a fini son service.
They finished cooking dinner.	Ils ont fini de cuisiner le repas du soir.

As we discussed earlier, for all regular verbs ending in "er" and "ir", you only have to conjuguate the verb "Avoir" (to have) followed by the verb you want to use. Find the root of the verb and then add the same termination each time.

How are you doing so far? Don't worry. We will keep working on this a little longer, using more examples.

Irregular past participles

Here you have a list of the most common verbs with irregular past particple. Memorize them, and you'll make your life with verbs so much easier.

English Verb	French Verb	Past participle
To can	**pouvoir**	pu
To want	**vouloir**	voulu
To have to /must	**devoir**	dû
To open	**ouvrir**	ouvert
To suffer	**souffrir**	souffert
To drive	**conduire**	Conduit
To build	**construire**	construit
To produce	**produire**	produit
To receive	**Recevoir**	reçu
To hold	**Tenir**	tenu
To believe	**croire**	cru
To lose	**perdre**	perdu

As with any other language, French is all about structure, and I promise it will get easier with some practice. As always, I will point other practical uses for this tense through the dialogue.

Undefined past

On the other side, in sentences using the imperfect past (passé imparfait), you never know when the action started or ended. It's the equivalent to say that "you used to" do something. You know it's not happening anymore, but can't really tell when it ended. With this being said, let's see some examples using the same verbs as before.

To travel	Voyager	Root	Termination
I traveled	Je voyageais		Er changes to "eais"
You traveled	Tu voyageais		Er changes to "eais"
He/She/It traveled	Il/Elle voyageait	Voyag-	Er changes to "eait"
We traveled	Nous voyagions		Er changes to "ions"
You traveled	Vous voyagiez		Er changes to "iez"

They traveled	Ils/Elles voyageaient		Er changes to "eaient"

Do you see what we did there? For conjugating regular verbs, you need to spot the root of the verb and then shift the termination, according to each case. For the verb "voyager", the root is "voyag-". For the verb "aimer" (to like), the root is "aim-". And for the verb "former" (to form), we have to employ the root "form-".

The same thing will happen for most of the verbs ending in "er", as in "manger" (root "mang-") or "chanter" (root "chant-"), and for the "ir" termination group, as in partir" (root "par-") or "réléchir" (root "réfléch-").

Come on! It may look hard, but it is not really that awful. You just need some practice and a few pointers, like the ones we discussed.

I traveled all the time, until I lost my passport.	Je voyageais tout le temps, jusqu'à ce que je perde mon passeport.
She traveled the continent while he was getting his degree.	Elle voyageait à travers le continent pendant qu'il passait son diplôme.

You traveled before having kids.	Vous voyagiez avant d'avoir des enfants.
We traveled every two months.	Nous voyagions tous les deux mois.

Notice how in these last sentences, you could have used "used to travel" instead of "traveled". This is important because it works as a hint—every time you can change an English verb in the past tense for a "used to + verb", you are in the presence of French imperfect past, and therefore all changes apply as we just practiced.

I used to travel all the time until I lost my passport.	Je voyageais tout le temps, jusqu'à ce que je perde mon passeport.
She used to travel the continent, while he was getting his degree.	Elle voyageait à travers le continent pendant qu'il passait son diplôme.
You used to travel before having kids.	Vous voyagiez avant d'avoir des enfants.
We used to travel every two months.	Nous voyagions tous les deux mois.

Are you getting better with your phrasing? Let's keep working.

To eat	Manger	Root	Termination
I ate	Je mangeais	Mang-	Er changes to "eais"
You ate	Tu mangeais		Er changes to "eais"
He/She ate	Il/Elle mangeait		Er changes to "eait"
We ate	Nous mangions		Er changes to "ions"
You ate	Vous mangiez		Er changes to "iez"
They ate	Ils mangeaient		Er changes to "eaient"

As always, don't worry. Practice makes perfect and in no time, you will have each tense covered. Let's keep practicing.

You ate an entire cake while I was watching TV.	Tu mangeais un gâteau en entier pendant que je regardais la télé.

She ate one piece of cake after dinner every night.	Elle mangeait un morceau de gâteau tous les soirs après le diner.
We ate one piece every time we saw each other.	Nous en mangions à chaque fois qu'on se voyait.
That night, they ate with so much joy!	Cette nuit-là, ils mangeaient avec tant de joie !

How is this sounding to you? Is it making any sense? Let's see more verbs.

To discover	**Descubrir**	**Root**	**Termination**
I discovered	Je découvrais	Decouvr-	Ir changes to "ais"
You discovered	Tu découvrais		Ir changes to "ais"
He/She/ discovered	Il/Elle découvrait		Ir changes to "ait"
We discovered	Nous découvrions		Ir changes to "ions"

You discovered	Vous découvriez		Ir changes to "iez"
They discovered	Ils/Elles découvraient		Ir changes to "aient"

Can you see how the terminations shift? Let's see some examples.

I discovered new ways before that happened.	Je découvrais de nouvelles façons, avant que cela n'arrive.
You discovered new ways to surprise me, night after night.	Tu découvrais de nouvelles façons de me surprendre, nuit après nuit.
She discovered a mark, and then another.	Elle découvrait une tâche, puis une autre.
They discovered what happened, until you found out.	Ils découvraient ce qui s'était passé, jusqu'à ce que tu l'apprennes.

See? It can get easier, quick. Let's go to our next verb: the irregular "to have", or "Avoir".

To have	Avoir
I had	J'avais
You had	Tu avais
He/She had	Il/Elle avait
We had	Nous avions
You had	Vous aviez
They had	Ils/Elles avaient

I had everything I could wish for.	J'avais tout ce que je désirais.
She had every opportunity.	Elle avait toutes les opportunités.
You had other plans, and it worked.	Tu avais d'autres plans et ça marchait.
We had so much to do.	Nous avions tellement de choses à faire.

Pay attention to the next verb. The verb "to be" is also an option when building sentences that are more complex. This turns it into a necessary tool to have in order to tell a great story.

To be	**être**
I was	J'étais
You were	Tu étais
He/She was	Il/Elle était
We were	Nous étions
You were	Vous étiez
They were	Ils/Elles étaient

Let's practice a bit more.

I was a Prom Queen.	J'étais la reine du bal.
He was a great athlete.	Il était un grand athlète.
We were a great team.	Nous étions une équipe formidable.
They were invincible.	Ils étaient invincibles.

After all those "different" pasts, you might be a little confused. Don't worry, I am going to present you two verbal forms that will save your life! Those require little to no conjugation and will allow you to express yourself in the most common situations.

1. Le présent progressif - the present progressive

It could be compared to the present continuous in English. It forms with the verb to be in the present and the expression "in train from/to" + verb to infinitive.

Examples:

What are you doing? I'm working.	Tu fais quoi ? Je suis en train de travailler.
Have you finished writing the letter? We are finishing.	Tu as fini d'écrire la lettre ? Nous sommes en train de finir.
Did he go to the grocery store? He is shopping right now.	Est-il allé au supermarché? Il est en train de faire les courses maintenant.
They are taking a test in classroom A.	Ils sont en train de passer une évaluation dans la salle A.

2. Le passé récent - The recent past

To express an action in the past that is close to the moment we speak, we use the verb « venir » in the present + de/d* + verb without conjugation.

At this time, I am sure that you already know how to conjugate the verb « venir » at the present tense, but just in case, here you have it once again.

Examples :

I just phoned my mother	Je viens d'appeler ma mère.
You have just arrived	Tu viens d'arriver.
He just arrived at the party.	Il vient d'arriver à la fête.
We just had dinner.	Nous venons de dîner.
The train has just left.	Le train vient de partir.

Through our dialogue, you will have the chance to see how all these elements fit together.

Kate: *Hello! I am so glad you came back from your trip. When did you arrive?*

Salut! Je suis tellement contente que tu sois revenue de ton voyage. Quand es-tu arrivé?

Alex: *Hi! I am glad as well. It was a fun trip. I've just arrived.*

Salut! Moi aussi. C'était un voyage sympathique. Je viens d'arriver.

Kate: *Great! Tell me!*

Super! Racontes-moi!

Alex: *Remember how I used to love rain?*

Tu te rappelles comme j'aimais la pluie?

Kate: *Of course.*

Bien-sûr.

Alex: *It turns out it was raining in Paris, but I had bought tickets to see a movie.*

Il s'est avéré qu'il pleuvait à Paris, mais j'avais acheté des billets pour aller regarder un film.

Kate: *Such a pity!*

C'est dommage!

Alex: *I have always had that thing with rain.*

J'ai toujours eu cette malchance avec la pluie.

Kate: *Indeed.*

Effectivement.

Alex: *It's fine, I still managed to visit a lot of places. The front desk agent gave me an umbrella.*

Ça va, j'ai quand même pu visiter beaucoup d'endroits. Le réceptionniste m'a donné un parapluie.

Kate: *Oh, that's nice!*

Oh, c'est gentil!

Alex: *You would love Paris, the food was delicious, I would love to go back.*

Tu adorerais Paris, la nourriture était délicieuse. J'adorerais y retourner.

Kate: *I've always wanted to go. We should plan a trip together!*

J'ai toujours voulue y aller. Nous devrions plannifier un voyage ensemble!

Alex: *Definitely! Have you finished your workday? We could grab a coffee and talk more.*

Certainement! Tu as fini ta journée de travail? On pourrait prendre un café et en parler.

Kate: *I am finishing one thing, but I can meet you in 5 minutes!*

Je suis en train de finir quelque chose mais je peux te rejoindre dans 5 minutes!

Alex: *Awesome! I will wait for you here.*

Super! Je t'attendrai ici.

Do you feel like an expert at putting phrases together? You should. We have come a long way. Besides, you are going to need those skills now because we are going on an adventure.

Chapter 6 – So Many Roads and So Many Places

I personally love to walk. When I was younger and single, I would put my earphones in and walk through any new city I got the chance to visit. Now, with my girlfriend, I put the headphones away and we enjoy long chats while walking and looking around. Sometimes she takes pictures, and they are mostly of me taking pictures of her or the landscape. But I enjoy watching her under all the different shades and lights. Have you ever noticed how every city has different colors and vibes?

Back to business. Tell me, what do you typically want to visit first when exploring a new city? Wherever you want to go, I am here to help you. Why don't we start with a few basics?

Museum	Musée
Where is the Louvres **Museum**?	Où se trouve le **musée** du Louvres?

Mu-zé

Square	Place
How can I get to Saint-Georges **Square**?	Comment puis-je me rendre à la **place** Saint-Georges?

Pla-ssuh

Avenue	Avenue
What can I find on the main **avenue**?	Que puis-je trouver sur l'**avenue** principale?

Ah-veh-nuh

This one should not be a problem. The pronunciation is very similar to the English "avenue".

Monuments	Monuments
Paris is rich in history and **monuments.**	Paris est riche en histoire et **monuments.**

Moh-nuh-men

Park	Parc
Park Buttes-Chaumont is in Paris.	Le **Parc** Buttes-Chaumont se situe à Paris.

Par-k

Church	Eglise
They gave me this **church** as a reference.	Ils m'ont donné cette **église** comme référence.

Ee-glee-zuh

Not to be disrespectful, but travelling is not just about history and monuments. It is also about having fun and experiencing the true local culture, as well as going to bars and clubs.

Bar	Bar
Where is this **bar**?	Où se trouve ce **bar**?

See? Globalization scores again!

Now that you have learned the name of some places, let's go there together.

Across	En face

| You can find them **across** the avenue. | Vous pouvez les trouver **en face** de l'avenue. |

En fah-suh

| In front of | Devant |
| He is waiting **in front of** the statue. | Il attends **devant** la statue. |

Deh-van

| Opposite | Opposé |
| We were walking in the **opposite** direction. | Nous étions en train de marcher du côté **opposé**. |

Oh-poo-zé

| Street | Rue |
| You can find it down the **street**. | Vous pouvez trouver ça en bas de la **rue**. |

ruh

| Subway | Métro |
| We can get there by **subway**. | Nous pouvons nous y rendre en **métro**. |

Meh-troh – This word comes from "Metropolitain" which as you can guess, means "Metropolitan".

Mall	Centre commercial
What kind of **mall** would you like to visit?	Quel type de **centre commercial** souhaiteriez-vous visiter?

Cen-truh ko-mer-sial

Recommend	Recommander
What can you **recommend?**	Qu'est-ce que vous **recommandez?**

Re-co-men-déh

"Recommander" is a general word for "suggestions". So, whenever you are out of ideas, just remember this one.

In terms of tourism, you should already be an expert at getting around. You learned how to request a cab, rent a car, and ask for directions and recommendations. You are almost done with this section, so why don't we practice a little more?

Front desk (Recepción): *Hello! How can I help you?*

Bonjour! Comment puis-je vous aider?

www.LearnLikeNatives.com

Allen: *I would like some recommendations for places to visit.*

J'aimerais avoir des recommandations d'endroits à visiter.

Front desk: *Very well. What type of place did you have in mind? A club, a museum?*

Très bien. Quel type d'endroit aviez-vous en tête? Un club, un musée?

Allen: *I heard that you have beautiful squares and monuments in this city.*

J'ai entendu que vous avez des places et des monuments magnifiques dans la ville.

Front desk: *That is true. Sadly, most cultural attractions are across town.*

C'est vrai. Malheureusement, la plupart des attractions touristiques sont de l'autre côté de la ville.

Philip: *Oh, I see. Could you give me some directions, please?*

	Oh, je vois. Pouvez-vous m'indiquer comment m'y rendre, s'il-vous-plaît?
Front desk:	*Sure! Would you like to travel by car or take the subway?*
	Bien-sûr! Vous préferez vous y rendre en voiture ou plutôt prendre le métro?
Philip:	*I would rather take a subway and walk.*
	Je préfèrerais prendre le métro et marcher.
Front desk:	*Very well. The subway is only 300m away.*
	Très bien. Le métro se trouve à seulement 300m d'ici.
Philip:	*Perfect! How do I get there?*
	Parfait! Comment puis-je m'y rendre?
Front desk:	*You only have to go down this street, take a right, and walk straight for 200m.*

	Vous avez seulement à descendre la rue, prendre à droite puis marcher tout droit pendant 200m.
Philip:	*That sounds easy. Thank you very much!*
	Ça à l'air facile. Merci beaucoup!
Front desk:	*All right, then. After you get to the subway, go to the mainline and take a train to étoile station.*
	D'accord, alors, en arrivant au métro, allez à la ligne principale et prenez le métro jusqu'à la station étoile.
Philip:	*Very good. I appreciate your help.*
	Très bien. Merci pour votre aide.
Front desk:	*My pleasure. Have a nice day.*
	Avec Plaisir. Bonne journée.
Allen:	*Likewise. Bye.*
	Egalement. Au revoir.

Ready to walk around the city and get lost in its little streets? I'm sure you can't wait. Then you'd better get ready. Go out and have fun. Who knows how many funny stories you will be able to tell once back from your trip!

Although now I am getting a bit hungry. Sorry, what did you say? Should we go and grab a bite to eat?

Chapter 7 – Eat, Travel, Love

Food is one of my favorite parts of traveling. Eating is an awesome way to learn a bit more about the culture and history of each place. Your nose and tongue become guides that can lead you through unknown passages, allowing you to enjoy the aromas of France in a glass of Cabernet; or to experience the culinary revolution in Paris, in the shape of a sweet and crusty croissant. Flavors are unique everywhere you go, and that is what makes them a huge part of traveling.

For this reason, I want to be sure I am giving you the opportunity to have the best experience. Plus, ordering food is a recurrent activity, which means you will have many chances to practice. I can also assure you something: some of the best typical food places will not have a translator. With that in mind, let's start this chapter.

Restaurant	Restaurant
Let's go into that **restaurant.**	Rentrons dans ce **restaurant.**

Rehs-to-ran

It is very similar to the English word, except for the intonation (Also, French people don't pronounce the "t" at the end.)

Table	Table
Table for four, please.	Une **table** pour quatre, s'il-vous-plaît.

Once again, the word is the same but the pronunciation is not. The French way to pronounce is: Tah-bluh".

Suggestions	Suggestions
Do you want to hear today's **suggestions?**	Vous voulez voir les **suggestions** du jour?

Suh-gest-eeon

Portion	Portion
I want a **portion** of fries.	J'aimerais avoir une **portion** de frites.

Pors-eeon

Quite easy, huh?

Fork	Fourchette
I dropped my **fork.**	J'ai fait tomber ma **fourchette.**

Foor-chett

Spoon	Cuillère
Can I get a **spoon**?	Puis-je avoir une **cuillère**?

Cu-ee-eh-ruh

Knife	Couteau
I will need a meat **knife.**	J'aurais besoin d'un **couteau** à viande.

Koo-toh

Plate	Assiette

| Can you bring an extra **plate**? | Pouvez-vous apporter une **assiette** en plus? |

Ass-ee-et

Entry	Entrée
Do you want an **entry**?	Voulez-vous une **entrée**?

An-tré

Main dish	Plat principal
For the **main dish**, I want the chicken.	En **plat principal**, j'aimerais le poulet.

Pla-prehn-si-pal

Well-cooked	Bien cuit
I want my steak **well-cooked**.	J'aimerais mon steak **bien cuit**.

Bee-n   koo-ee

"Bien" (Bee-n) means "good".

Medium	A point
Medium is fine for me.	**A point,** ça me convient.

Ah poo-ehn

Dessert	Dessert
Of course, I want a **dessert**.	Bien-sûr que j'aimerais avoir un **dessert**.

Deh-ssehr (The "s" is pronounced as "s", not as a "z", like the English way.)

Vegan	Végétalien
Do you have a vegan menu?	Est-ce que vous avez un menu **végétalien**?

Veh-geh-tal-ee-ehn (Note that French people also say "vegan" sometimes, so they will probably understand this word, especially in restaurants.)

Check	Addition
I want the **check**, please.	J'aimerais avoir l'**addition**, s'il-vous-plaît.

Ah-dee-ssion

Are you excited to order your first dish? Why don't we go practice a bit more first...

Waiter (serveur):	*Good afternoon! Welcome to our restaurant. My name is Shawn. How many are you?*
	Bonjour! Bienvenue dans notre restaurant. Mon nom est Shawn. Vous êtes combien?
Mike:	*Hello! We have a reservation under Paulson. Table for four.*
	Bonjour! Nous avons une réservation sous le nom de Paulson, table pour quatre.
Waiter:	*Yes, here you are. Come with me, please.*
	Oui, je vois. Venez avec moi, s'il-vous-plaît.
Mike:	*I would like to order right away. We are starving.*
	J'aimerais commander maintenant. Nous sommes morts de faim.
Waiter:	*Perfect. What would you like to order?*
	Parfait. Que voulez-vous commander?
Mike:	*What are your suggestions?*
	Quelles sont vos suggestions?

Waiter:	*The lobster ceviche as an appetizer. For the main dish, we have a beef tartare which is excellent.*
	Le ceviche de homard en entrée. En plat principal, nous avons un excellent tartare de boeuf.
Mike:	*Sounds great! I want one of each. Also, a salad and two beef dishes.*
	Ça a l'air fabuleux! Je voudrais un de chaque. Aussi, une salade et deux plats à base de boeuf.
Waiter:	*Do you want extra plates to share?*
	Vous voulez des assiettes pour partager?
Mike:	*Yes, please.*
	Oui, s'il-vous-plaît.
Waiter:	*Perfect. I will be back in a second with your plates, forks, and meat knives.*
	Parfait. Je reviens dans une seconde avec vos assiettes, fourchettes et couteaux à viande.

Mike: *Thank you very much.*

Merci beaucoup.

Waiter: *I'll be right back.*

Je reviens tout de suite.

I bet this chapter was easy. How did you feel after repeating that last dialogue? Look... I do not want to freak you out, but you are about to feel a bit under the weather.

Chapter 8 – Sick & Abroad!

Every time I travel abroad, I buy insurance, but the truth is I always hope I will not need it. Being sick can be scary, and no one likes to feel ill. Moreover, nobody wants it to interrupt their vacation! However, if you have to be prepared for something, this is definitely it. Great communication can be the key to solving major problems. So, let's get prepared.

Ill	Malade
I think I am **ill.**	Je crois que je suis **malade.**

Here we see the word "ma-lah-duh" again, I know, but it is very important.

Cold	Rhume
I think I caught a **cold**.	Je crois que j'ai attrapé un **Rhume**.

Ru-muh

Cough	Toux
I have a slight **cough**.	J'ai une petite **toux**.

Too

Pain	Douleur
I took something for the **pain**.	J'ai pris quelque chose pour la **douleur**.

Doo-leur

Migraine	Migraine
I have a **migraine**.	J'ai une **migraine**.

Mee-greh-nuh

Swollen	Gonflé
My throat is a bit **swollen**.	Ma gorge est un peu **gonflée**.

Gonf-leh

Call the doctor	Appeler le docteur
Do you want to call the **doctor**?	Est-ce que tu veux appeler le **docteur**?

Doc-tuhr

Emergency	Urgence
I have an **emergency.**	J'ai une **urgence.**

Ur-gen-ssuh

Feel	Sentir
I **feel** a bit better.	Je me **sens** un peu mieux.

Sen-teer

Patient	Patient
I am a **patient** of Dr. Castillo.	Je suis un **patient** du Dr. Castillo.

Pah-See-an

Blood pressure	Pression sanguine

| The **blood pressure** is fine. | La **pression sanguine** est bien. |

Preh-si-on san-ghee-nuh

| Pharmacy | Pharmacie |

| Where is the nearest **pharmacy**? | Où est la **pharmacie** la plus proche? |

Similar to English: "phar-ma-cee".

| Prescription | Ordonnance |

| I will need a **prescription**. | Je vais avoir besoin d'une **ordonnance**. |

Or-doh-naan-suh

| Pills | Comprimés |

| How many **pills** do I need? | Il me faut combien de **comprimés**? |

Com-pree-mé

We have already seen a similar scenario in a previous chapter, do you remember? So, this should be easy as we have covered it before. Are you ready to practice?

Liam: *Hello! I would like to speak to Dr. Castil.*

Bonjour ! J'aimerais parler au Dr. Castil.

Secretary (secretaire): *Good afternoon, Sir. What is your name?*

Bonjour, monsieur. Puis-je avoir votre nom ?

Liam: *I am Liam Smith. One of his patients.*

Je suis Liam Smith. Un de ses patients.

Secretary: *Good afternoon, sir. Why do you call today?*

Bonjour, monsieur. Quelle est la raison de votre appel ?

Liam: *I have an emergency. My youngest son has a strong headache.*

J'ai une urgence. Mon plus jeune fils a un gros mal de tête.

Secretary: *Any other symptoms?*

D'autres symptomes ?

Liam: 38°C fever. Also complaints of abdominal pain.

38°C de fièvre. Il se plaint de douleurs abdominales.

Secretary: Is he allergic to something?

Est-ce qu'il est allergique à quelque chose?

Liam: Yes. To gluten.

Oui. Au gluten.

Secretary: Is he taking any prescriptions?

Est-ce qu'il prends un traitement?

Liam: No, just a dietary supplement.

Non. Juste des complements alimentaires.

Secretary: Come here at once and bring those pills.

Venez ici au plus vite et prenez les comprimés.

Yeah, I know what you are thinking: no parent with a celiac kid would give him random pills! I feel you, but I have also seen it happen.

I sincerely hope this book will help you better understand and speak French. I love to travel and the diversity in people and styles, and I hope you enjoy the same things. I know how much independence and confidence you can gain by being able to communicate in more than one language. So, stay with me! We need you focused! Did I forget to mention something? You are now looking for a job.

Chapter 9 – Learn the Ropes

Looking for new employment can be both a frustrating and an exciting situation. I am used to working on my own–which allows me to travel more–but I still have to get my own clients. If you are relocating or just thinking of spending a season in another city, finding a job at a local business could be a great opportunity to get in touch with the culture from a closer perspective.

As always, I will try to keep it simple.

Employment	Emploi
I am looking for **employment.**	Je cherche un **emploi.**

Am-plwah

Employer	Employeur
My **employer** is very nice.	Mon **employeur** est très gentil.

Am-plwah-yur

Employee	Employé

| I am an **employee** of this shop. | Je un **employé** de ce magasin. |

Am-plwah-yé

| Permanent position | Emploi permanent |
| I would like a **permanent position**. | J'aimerai un **emploi permanent**. |

Am-plwa pehr-mah-naan

| Temporary job | Emploi temporaire |
| I have a **temporary job**. | J'ai un **emploi temporaire**. |

Trah-bah-joh-tem-po-rahl

| Salary | Salaire |
| I want a **salary** increase. | Je veux une augmentation de **salaire**. |

First and last name are very common expressions, and so far, you must have used it a dozen times. However, we will need it to write your CV, so just in case...

| First name | Prénom |

| What is your **first name**? | Quel est votre **prénom**? |

Pré-nom

| Last name | Nom de famille |
| My **last name** is Dubois. | Mon **nom de famille** est Dubois. |

As you can surely guess, "nom de famille" means "family name".

Nom-duh-fa-mee

| Profession | Profession |
| What is your **profession**? | Quelle est votre **profession**? |

Pro-phé-ssion

| Credentials | Justificatifs |
| Here are my **credentials.** | Voici mes **justificatifs.** |

Ju-stee-fee-cah-teef

| Skills | Compétences |

| These are my main **skills**. | Voici mes **compétences** principales. |

Com-pé-tan-suh

As we know, the job market is different from how it was years ago. For many companies around the world, degrees and qualifications are not as important as they used to be. Therefore, a complete list of your knowledge and skills is very important.

| Job title | Titre de poste |
| My **job title** is Manager. | Mon **titre de poste** est responsable. |

Tit-ruh duh pos-tuh

| Job description | Description de poste |
| That is not under my **job description.** | Cela n'est pas dans ma **description de poste.** |

Des-krip-see-on-the-post

Your job description is, of course, crucial. While your job title might say something, your job description should provide a specific idea of what is expected from you.

Milestone	Jalon
What is your favorite **milestone?**	Quel est ton **jalon** preferée?

Jah-lon

As we already said, where you worked in the past and for how long it doesn't matter anymore. What truly matters is what you have accomplished in the past. Choose wisely your greatest "jalon" to prove your skills.

Manager	Responsable
Congratulations! You are the new **manager.**	Felicitations! Vous êtes le nouveau **responsable.**

Rés-pon-sah-bluh

Congratulations! I am so happy for you!

That escalated quickly, huh?

You know my motto: practice makes perfect! Let's dive into our next dialogue.

Manager (responsable): *Hello! What can I do for you?*

	Bonjour! Que puis-je faire pour vous?
Owen:	*Hello! I am looking for employment.*
	Bonjour! Je recherche un emploi.
Manager	*What is your name?*
	Quel est votre nom?
Owen:	*Owen Miller.*
	Owen Miller.
Manager	*Very well. What type of work are you looking for?*
	Très bien. Quel type de travail recherchez-vous?
Owen:	*I would like anything. Even a temporary job.*
	J'aimerais n'importe lequel. Même un emploi temporaire.
Manager	*Right. Did you bring your CV?*
	D'accord. Avez-vous votre amené CV?
Owen:	*Yes. Here it is.*

	Oui. Le voici.
Manager	*Very good. What are your major skills?*
	Très bien? Quelles sont vos principales compétences?
Owen:	*I am good at logo design.*
	Je suis doué en conception de logo.
Manager	*What are your most relevant milestones from the past year?*
	Quels sont vos jalons les plus pertinents de l'année dernière?
Owen:	*I won campaigns for logo refreshments in 5 major companies.*
	J'ai gagné des campagnes pour l'élaboration de nouveaux logos dans 5 grandes entreprises.
Manager	*All right. We will call you for another interview.*
	D'accord. Nous vous appelerons pour un autre entretien.

Owen:	*Do you have any vacancies?*
	Vous avez des postes vacants?
Manager	*We have a job for a designer. It could turn into a permanent position.*
	Nous avons un projet pour un designer. Cela pourrait devenir un poste permanent.
Owen:	*That is great.*
	C'est super.
Manager	*Yes, it is. You would get entry salary plus bonuses.*
	Oui. Vous toucheriez un salaire de base, plus des bonus.
Owen:	*Awesome. I will wait for your call.*
	Genial. J'attends votre appel.

We already had a little walkthrough for an interview, but we will work harder on that in the next chapter. After all, we have to get you ready for your first big job.

Chapter 10 – Bring, Learn & Lead

As the title of this chapter suggests, now is the time to bring, learn and lead, because you have to shine in your job interview. This is the time to talk about your ambition, show how good you are at planning and projecting, and demonstrate why you will be a great fit. To do so, we will need to introduce a new tense: the future.

As you will see, the future is formed by the infinitive of the verb (and not the root) plus the termination of the future, which is the same for all the 3 conjugations. Amazing right?

First verb: "to bring" – "apporter". As you will see, we'll take the infinitive "apporter" and we all add the terminations:

Ah-por-té

To bring	Apporter	Infinitive	Termination
I will bring	J'apporterai		Add "ai"
You will bring	Tu apporteras	Apporter-	Add "as"
He/She/It will bring	Il/elle apportera		Add "a"

We will bring	Nous apperterons		Add "ons"
You will bring	Vous apporterez		Add "ez"
They will bring	Ils/elles apporteront		Add "ont"

The good thing is that a job interview comes down to talking mostly about yourself. Therefore, it is important to know all the conjugations before you talk about your plans for specific people or other departments. The main goal, however, is learning to talk about yourself.

J' ah-por-tuh-réh

Now, let's go through examples.

I will bring all my experience.	J'apporterai toute mon experience.
He will bring many resources.	Il apportera beaucoup de ressources.

We will bring a new selling strategy.	Nous apporterons une nouvelle stratégie de vente.
They will bring everything we need §for this project.	Ils apporteront tout ce dont nous avons besoin pour ce projet.

With verbs ending in -RE, things work the same way, but you just have to remember to drop the -E of the infinitive before adding the termination of the future.

For exemple, with the verb "aprendre", you remove the last -E

To learn	Apprendre	Infinitive (without -e)	Termination
I will learn	J'apprendrai	Aprendr-	Add "ai"
You will learn	Tu apprendras		Add "as"
He/She will learn	Il/elle apprendra		Add "a"

We will learn	Nous apprendrons		Add "ons"
You will learn	Vous apprendrez		Add "ez"
They will learn	Ils/Elles apprendront		Add "ont"

Again, let's take a moment to focus on you: ah-pren-dré.

I will learn in this company.	J'apprendrai au sein de cette compagnie.
He will learn from this experience.	Il apprendra de cette expérience.
We will learn through hard work.	Nous apprendrons en travaillant dur.
They will learn a lot.	Ils apprendront beaucoup.

From a hiring perspective, "to lead" is a very important verb. Being able to lead is a well-appreciated skill for most recruiters, especially for some positions.

To lead	Diriger	Infinitive	Termination
I will lead	Je dirigerai	Diriger-	Add "ai"
You will lead	Tu dirigeras		Add "as"
He/She will lead	Il/Elle dirigera		Add "a"
We will lead	Nous dirigerons		Add "ons"
You will lead	Vous dirigerez		Add "án"
They will lead	Ils/Elles dirigeront		Add "án"

Guh-dee-ree-guh-reh

You will lead this project.	Tu dirigeras ce projet.
She will lead this department.	Ella dirigera ce département.
We will lead the first part of the conference.	Nous dirigerons la première partie de la conference.

| They will lead us to success. | Ils nous dirigeront vers le succès. |

The next verb to look at is the verb "to be". It is with this verb that I first learned the auxiliary for the future (will) and its uses. More than that, it gives you a basic structure for putting sentences together in the "futur simple", the most commonly used tense for the future.

To be	Ser
I will be	Je serai
You will be	Tu seras
He/She will be	Elle sera
We will be	Nous serons
You will be	Vous serez
They will be	Ils seront

First, let's practice with the future tense of "être".

I will be the leader in this project.	Je serai le dirigeant de ce projet
He will be a great asset to this team.	Il sera un grand atout pour cette équipe
This software will be great for us.	Ce programme sera super pour nous.
They will take care of everything.	Ils se chargeront de tout.

You can see that for French, the words "will be" compress to form a simple idea: "je serai". This is the French form for "to be" that will happen in the future.

With this, you can create sentences talking about what you have planned for the future.

"With these changes, we will be the first company in our field."

"Avec ces changements, nous serons la première compagnie dans notre domaine."

Now, let's check our final verb, "Avoir". (be careful, it's irregular)

To have	Avoir
I will have	J'aurai
You will have	Tu auras
He/She will have	Il/Elle aura
We will have	Nous aurons
You will have	Vous aurez
They will have	Ils auront

Another form of future which is also used quite often is the "futur proche", the "near future".

As for the past(with the Passé recent), this is your life jacket whenever you want to talk about the future. This form of future requires the conjugation knowledge of only one verb, which will fit for all. Let's see how this works:

The « futur proche » is formed by the verb « Aller » - « to go » in the present, followed by a verb with the infinitive.

Here's the conjugation of « to go », in French :

To go	Aller

I go	Je vais
You go	Tu vas
He/She goes	Il/Elle va
We go	Nous allons
You go	Vous allez
They go	Ils vont

Let's practice with some examples :

Look, it is going to rain !	Regardes ! Il va pleuvoir
I am going to do some shopping.	Je vais faire quelques achats.
You are going to travel next week.	Tu vas voyager la semaine prochaine.
We are going to sleep now.	Nous allons dormir maintenant.

Yes. I can almost hear you talking. No worries. We will see more of these examples in the next dialogue.

Mr. King:	*Hello. Are you Leo Mitchell?*
	Bonjour, êtes-vous Leo Mitchell?
Leo:	*Good afternoon. Yes, I am.*
	Bonjour. Oui, c'est moi.
Mr. King:	*Perfect. Please, come with me.*
	Parfait. Venez avec moi, s'il-vous-plaît.
Leo:	*Sure.*
	D'accord.
Mr. King:	*Tell me, Leo. If we hire you, what will you bring to the company?*
	Dites-moi, Leo. Si on vous embauche, qu'est-ce-que vous apporterez à l'entreprise?
Leo:	*I will bring 10-year experience in conflict and risks management.*

	J'apporterai 10 ans d'experience en management de conflits et risques.
Mr. King:	*According to your knowledge, when will the updates be made?*
	Selon votre expérience, quand pourrez-vous mettre en place les changements?
Leo:	*I will have updates done within the first semester of 2020.*
	Je les mettrai en place le premier semester de 2020.
Mr. King:	*What will you need to achieve that?*
	De quoi aurez-vous besoin pour y parvenir?
Leo:	*I will need a team, including two technicians.*
	J'aurais besoin d'une équipe, incluant deux techniciens.
Mr. King	*Very well. When can you start?*
	Très bien. Quand pouvez-vous commencer?
Leo:	*Next week works for me.*

La semaine prochaine me va bien.

Mr. King   *Great. I am going to arrange an office for you.*

Super. Je vais m'organiser pour vous trouver un bureau.

Leo: *Thank you very much. And I am going to prepare for my first day as much as I can.*

Merci beaucoup. Et moi je vais me préparer pour mon premier jour autant que possible.

I hope you are cracking this. All languages are about structure and, even if some are more complex than others, they become natural with time and practice. By the way, have you had a look at your new office?

www.LearnLikeNatives.com

Chapter 11 – New Job, New Life

I always feel a bit uncomfortable the first time I am in a new place, especially if it is going to be my new work environment! Of course, I also think it's great to meet new people, build friendships and more generally have the chance to network with other peers.

You won't have to worry as we are here to prepare you for what is coming. Do you want to join me?

Please, join me in your new office.

Office	Bureau
This is your **office.**	Voici votre **bureau.**

Bu-ro

Computer	Ordinateur
Your **computer** is ready to use.	Votre **ordinateur** est prêt à être utilisé.

Database	Base de données
I granted you access to this **database.**	Je vous ai donné l'accès à cette **base de données.**

Bah-se-the-do-né

Software	Programme
We have the best **software** to manage our database.	Nous avons le meilleur **programme** pour gérer notre base de données.

Pro-gra-muh

Keyboard	Clavier
This is a nice **keyboard.**	Celui-ci est un bon **clavier.**

Kla-vee-eh

Monitor	Écran

| I need a larger **monitor**. | J'ai besoin d'un **écran** plus grand. |

Eh-kran

| Mouse | Souris |
| My **mouse** is ergonomic. | Ma **souris** est ergonomique. |

Soo-ree

| Hard drive | Disque dur |
| That is a 2 terabyte **hard drive**. | C'est un **disque dur** de 2 terabytes. |

This-cuh-duh-ruh

| File | Dossier |
| You will find all you need in the **file**. | Vous trouverez tout ce dont vous avez besoin dans le **dossier**. |

Fee-chee-eh

| Document | Document |
| I already sent that **document**. | J'ai déja envoyé ce **document**. |

Do-cu-men

Report	Rapport
I will send the **report** this afternoon.	J'enverrai le **rapport** cet après-midi.

Ra-por

Coordinate	Coordonner
We need to **coordinate** that meeting.	Nous devons **coordonner** cette reunion.

Ko-or-di-neh

Desk	Bureau
This is a nice **desk.**	C'est un joli **bureau.**

Bu-ro

In French, we use the same word to talk about an office and a desk.

Department	Departement
I work for the Human Resources **department.**	Je travaille pour le **departement** des Ressources humaines.

Dé-par-tuh-men

Coworker	Collègue (de travail)
I had lunch with a **coworker.**	J'ai déjeuné avec un **collègue.**

Ko-leh-guh

Are you eager to practice? Great! Let's do this!

Eli: *How do you like your new office?*

Tu aimes bien ton nouveau bureau?

Jace: *I like it a lot. I think I will need another monitor to split screens.*

J'aime beaucoup. Je pense que j'aurai besoin d'un autre écran.

Eli: *Most coworkers do. We can coordinate that with the IT Department.*

La plupart des collègues en ont deux. On peut coordonner ça avec le service technique.

Jace: *Perfect. Thank you. I love my desk.*

| | Parfait. Merci. J'adore mon bureau. |

Eli: Yes. We invest in computers, software, and great equipment.

Oui. Nous investissons dans des ordinateurs, des logiciels et du bon équipement.

Jace: When are you expecting to have the files you requested?

Quand avez-vous besoin des dossiers que vous avez demandé?

Eli: Tomorrow is fine.

Demain, c'est bon.

Jace: Good. I just have to add a few documents.

D'accord. Je dois juste rajouter quelques documents.

Eli: Great, Jace! I think you will be a great addition to our team.

Génial, Jace! Je pense que tu sera un très bon attribut pour notre équipe.

Jace: *Thank you for trusting in me. I will not let you down*

Merci de me faire confiance. Je ne vous décevrai pas.

How was your first day on the job? Are you already familiar with the coffee machine? You'd better work hard as you are going to be very busy soon.

www.LearnLikeNatives.com

A Quick Message

A quick message before we start the final chapter of this book.

"No one can whistle a symphony. It takes a whole orchestra to play it." –

H.E. Luccock

Do you want to be part of the orchestra of the Learning French community?

Here is how:

If you're enjoying this book, I would like to kindly ask you to leave a brief review on Amazon.

Reviews aren't easy to come by, but they have a profound impact in supporting my work. This way, I can keep creating new content to help the whole community at my very best.

I would be incredibly thankful if you could just take a minute to leave a quick review on Amazon, even if it's just a sentence or two!

It's that simple!

Thank you so much for taking the time to leave a short review on Amazon.

The community and I are very appreciative, as your review makes a difference.

Now, let's get back to learning French!

www.LearnLikeNatives.com

Chapter 12 – Bringing Home the Bacon

You have been preparing for this moment. You got yourself a new job, you have a new office and work team, and now is the time to start closing some business and bringing home the money. As always, let's first go with the essentials.

Meeting	Réunion
We have everything ready for the **meeting**.	Tout est prêt pour la **reunion**.

Re-u-nion

Sell	Vendre
We plan to **sell** when it reaches $95.	Nous plannifions de **vendre** quand il atteint $95.

Ven-druh

Take your time to practice that final "r" sound.

Capital	Capital

| We need to raise **capital.** | Nous devons augmenter le **capital.** |

Ka-pi-tal

Market	Marché
The **market** is shifting.	Le **marché** est en train de changer.

Mar-sheh

Stock market	Bourse
The **stock market** could crash.	La **bourse** pourrait s'éffondrer.

Boor-suh

Project	Projet
The new **project** is very complex.	Le nouveau **projet** est très complexe.

Pro-jeh

Budget	Budget
The available **budget** is 750k.	Le **budget** disponible est de 750 mille.

Bud-jé

Presentation	Présentation
I'll have the **presentation** ready by 1 pm.	La **presentation** sera prête à 13h.

Pre-sen-ta-sion

Supply	Offre
The **supply** is decreasing for some commodities.	L'**offre** diminue pour certains produits.

Off-ruh

Demand	Demande
The people **demand** new solutions.	Les gens **demandent** de nouvelles solutions.

De-man-duh

Experience	Expérience
I have 7 years of professional **experience.**	J'ai 7 ans d'**expérience** professionnelle.

Ex-pe-riehn-suh

| Invoice | Facture |

| I will send you my **invoice.** | Je vous enverrai ma **facture.** |

Fact-u-ruh

| Credit | Crédit |
| They have great **credit.** | Ils ont un superbe **crédit.** |

Cré-di

Just like the English word, but you don't pronounce the "t".

| Loan | Emprunt |
| I will pay half of the **loan.** | Vous payerez la moitié de **l'emprunt.** |

Am-prun

| Taxes | Taxes |
| I have to calculate my **taxes.** | Je dois calculer mes **taxes.** |

Tax-uh

| Investment | Investissement |
| It is a great **investment.** | C'est un super **investissement.** |

Ein-ves-tis-uh-man

Spend	Dépenser
It is important to **spend** in quality.	C'est important de **dépenser** en qualité.

Dé-pan-sé

Save	Economiser
We can **save** up to 30%.	Nous pouvons **économiser** jusqu'à 30%.

E-ko-no-mi-zé

Lose	Perdre
Sometimes you need to **lose**.	Parfois, tu dois **perdre**.

Per-druh

Here we are. This is the final test. This chapter's practice is meant to gather general knowledge from the last three chapters. Are you ready to buckle? Don't be scared. You got this.

Mr. Reed : *I am going to be clear. I want a company to protect my investment.*

	Je vais être clair. Je veux une compagnie pour protéger mon investissement.
Mr. Evans:	*Perfect. I can offer you all my experience for that job.*
	Parfait. Je peux vous offrir toute mon expérience pour ce travail.
Mr. Reed:	*What will be your strategy?*
	Quelle sera votre stratégie?
Mr. Evans:	*You have good credit. I plan to use a loan and increase the supply.*
	Vous avez un bon crédit. Je compte utiliser un prêt et augmenter l'offre.
Mr. Reed:	*How will I save capital that way?*
	Comment je vais économiser du capital comme ça?
Mr. Evans:	*By covering for the demand, I expect a rise in the Stock Market.*
	En couvrant la demande. J'attends une hausse de la bourse.

Mr. Reed:	*That will not do it alone.*
	Ça ne fera pas l'affaire.
Mr. Evans:	*I know. That is why we have a strategy to increase our market share by 3%.*
	Je sais. C'est pourquoi nous avons une stratégie pour augmenter notre part de marché de 3%.
Mr. Reed:	*Very well. I expect that you will have a great presentation for my board meeting.*
	Très bien. J'attends que vous fassiez une superbe presentation pour le conseil d'administration.
Mr. Evans:	*You know I will. My budget projections do not lie.*
	Vous savez bien que oui. Mes projections de budget ne mentent pas.
Mr. Reed:	*All right. I expect your invoice, then.*
	Très bien. J'attends votre facture alors.
Mr. Evans:	*I will be sending it tomorrow.*

Je vous l'enverrai demain.

I would like to get your opinion. How was this chapter for you? And now ask yourself: how could you improve your knowledge? As I have been saying from the beginning, you will be able to learn the language by repeating all the lessons in this book. And practice is the only way to do it—repeat it all out will help a lot.

Conclusion

Congratulations on making it through to the end of this book! You now have all the tools you need to achieve your French goals.

This is no science. Of course, there is a method, but it is mostly practicing, repeating, and doing! So, go for it. If you find yourself feeling unsure about something, just come back and look it up, and we'll go through it together! Yet, I am sure you already know so much, even more than you realize!

Look at all the things we did: we learned how to plan a trip, we discussed how to act if you or your family get sick, reviewed how to move around the city, ask for directions, and we had a nice conversation about how to talk about the past and the future.

We also learned how to deal with business in French: we talked about how to present a CV and become an employee. Also, we went through some commercial and business French to help you make great deals if you find yourself covering a management position.

Do you realize all the new things you can communicate now? You now have more resources for survival and regular living in a completely new environment, and I want to give you a big pat on the back for coming this far.

You can find the rest of the books in the series, as well as a whole host of other resources, at **LearnLikeNatives.com**. Simply add the book to your library to take the next step in your language learning journey. If you are ever in need of new ideas or direction, refer to our 'Speak Like a Native' eBook, available to you for free at **LearnLikeNatives.com**, which clearly outlines practical steps you can take to continue learning any language you choose.

Nevertheless, did I mention we are not over yet?

Now the fun part begins: try to watch your favorite cartoons in French, or try with some famous TV series, of course with French subtitles (yes French subtitles, you can make it!). If you like french movies, why not watch a Louis de Funès movie? They're big classics and fun to follow, yet extremely helpful for improving your French!

Again, thank you for listening. I hope to meet you in the near future so we can learn even more!

www.LearnLikeNatives.com

www.LearnLikeNatives.com

Learn Like a Native is a revolutionary **language education brand** that is taking the linguistic world by storm. Forget boring grammar books that never get you anywhere, Learn Like a Native teaches you languages in a fast and fun way that actually works!

As an international, multichannel, language learning platform, we provide **books, audio guides and eBooks** so that you can acquire the knowledge you need, swiftly and easily.

Our **subject-based learning**, structured around real-world scenarios, builds your conversational muscle and ensures you learn the content most relevant to your requirements. Discover our tools at *LearnLikeNatives.com*

When it comes to learning languages, we've got you covered!

www.ingramcontent.com/pod-product-compliance
Lightning Source LLC
Chambersburg PA
CBHW070044120526
44589CB00035B/2307